My Body

Neil Wilson

Acknowledgements

Folens allows photocopying of selected pages for educational use, providing that this use is within the confines of the purchasing institution. Copiable pages should not be declared in any return in respect of any photocopying licence.

Folens books are protected by international copyright laws. All rights are reserved. The copyright of all materials in this book, except where otherwise stated, remains the property of the publisher and author. No part of this publication may be reproduced, stored in a retrieval system, or transmitted, in any form or by any means, for whatever purpose, without the written permission of Folens Limited.

This resource may be used in a variety of ways. However, it is not intended that teachers or children should write directly into the book itself.

Neil Wilson hereby asserts his moral right to be identified as the author of this work in accordance with the Copyright, Designs and Patents Act 1988.

Illustrations: Sutton Ziaian, Cambridge   Cover design: John Hawkins, Design for Marketing

© 1994 Folens Limited, on behalf of the author.
Reprinted 1997.

First published 1994 by Folens Limited, Dunstable and Dublin.
Folens Limited, Albert House, Apex Business Centre, Boscombe Road, Dunstable, LU5 4RL, United Kingdom.

ISBN 1 85276 417-1

Printed in Singapore by Craft Print.

Contents

Introduction	4
Teachers' notes	5

Skeleton, bones and joints

My body	6
My bones	7
My joints	8
Which joints are where?	9
Joints I use when I'm ...	10
Making a model with joints	11

Brain

How your brain gets information	12
Your brain	13
Helping your memory	14
Memory fun	15

Airways and breathing

Respiration	16
Measuring your lung capacity	17
Keeping your lungs clean	18
Breathing	19
Checking your breathing	20
Coughs and colds	21
Lungs and smoking	22
Resource Sheet: Lungs and smoking	23
Smoking	24

Digestion

Where does your food go?	25
Resource Sheet: Where does your food go?	26
Putting your organs in place	27
Resource Sheet: Putting your organs in place	28
Cleaning your blood	29

Heart and pulse

Your heart	30
Your pulse	31

Muscles

Muscles	32
Making a model arm	33
Strength	34

Skin

Fingerprints	35
Looking at skin	36
Resource Sheet: Looking at skin	37
Keeping warm and keeping cool	38
Cuts and infections	39

Teeth

Teeth	40
The tooth test: What's your score?	41

Senses

The sense of touch	42
Protect your ears	43
Using your ears	44
Looking at eyes	45
Why do we have two eyes?	46
Your tongue	47
Your nose	48

© 1994 Folens Ltd.

Introduction

My Body, as part of the Getting Personal series, is designed to support teachers of 9-11 year olds in their teaching of the cross-curricular Health Education theme. It may be used as a self-contained unit, or in conjunction with other materials, particularly when children are learning about living things as part of the Science curriculum.

It must be recognised that there are many influences on a child's developing attitude to health: family, peer group, community and the media. However, schools can have a strong influence on the development of a healthy lifestyle for their children by providing accurate information within a coherently developed health education curriculum.

The activities in this book are designed to introduce pupils to, or reinforce their knowledge of, the major organs and systems of the body, nutrition, support, movement and lifestyle. They encourage the exploration of ideas about the processes of breathing, growth, digestion and circulation. Active questioning and the use of discussion points lead the children to consider how to keep their bodies healthy: the need for suitable food, exercise and personal hygiene, and the damage which may be caused by harmful habits such as smoking and a general lack of care. Also considered are care for the environment and environmental effects on people's health.

The activities provided in *My Body* help children to become aware of the similarities between all humans, and also of the differences. They are presented in a way which promotes a positive attitude to the body and the acceptance that we are all different, but neither 'better' nor 'worse' because of the differences.

Many children come from families where the promotion of a healthy lifestyle is not a priority, or where economic, cultural and religious factors affect their attitudes to food and exercise. Teachers need to approach this sensitively, perhaps by keeping parents informed of forthcoming studies, and by inviting their comments.

Note: Charts and graphs appear throughout the book for children's guidance. A jagged edge indicates an incomplete chart: children can be encouraged to explore additional ideas of their own.

Teachers' notes

Skeleton, bones and joints - pages 6-11
This section begins with basic activities which involve labelling parts of the body and skeleton. Teachers could develop these activities into research tasks by encouraging pupils to find out the correct anatomical terms for the different parts, such as mandible, patella, etc.
When attempting the 'Which joints are where?' activity, make sure that the felt tip pens used by the pupils are water-soluble!

Brain - pages 12-15
'How your brain gets information' introduces pupils to how the brain uses the information it receives from the different senses. The brain is a vital organ and 'Your brain' explains to pupils the importance of protecting it, especially during play (roller-skating, skateboards, playgrounds, bicycles are all potential hazards), and defines in broad terms the parts of the brain which control the different parts of the body. 'Helping your memory' and 'Memory fun' are practical aids to improve memory.

Airways and breathing - pages 16-24
This section is devoted to lungs, breathing and respiration. Air quality is examined, the importance to life of oxygen, and the dangers of smoking.
Pupils are encouraged to investigate their lung capacity, and their breathing and pulse rates at rest and after exercise.
The connection between clean air and good health should be highlighted.

Digestion - pages 25-29
The activities focus on encouraging pupils' awareness of the function of some internal organs. Teachers could bring in some examples from a butcher.
Extension work could include drawing.

 Plastic gloves should be worn when handling these organs. Hands should be washed thoroughly afterwards.

Role play: invite the children to enact the journey a piece of food makes through the body's organs.

Heart and pulse - pages 30-31
Listening to the heart beat, measuring pulse rates and looking at how pulse rate is affected by exercise are approached through practical activities. Extension exercises could include an analysis of class leisure-time activities which involve exercise, and looking at how recovery rate is an indication of fitness.

Muscles - pages 32-34
This section continues the theme of exercise and how it can increase muscle strength. Pupils should enjoy the flexibility exercises.

 Before attempting flexibility exercises, children must warm up, e.g. by jogging on the spot for three minutes.

The model arm exercise will help pupils to understand how muscles help to move bones, and how the thickness of the muscle helps to determine strength.

Skin - pages 35-39
Pupils have the opportunity to take a detailed look at skin, and do some model making. They make skin prints, examine skin's reaction to temperature, and learn how to prevent cuts becoming infected.

Teeth - pages 40-41
This section discusses the contribution of sugar to tooth decay. Pupils are encouraged to examine different types of food to discover how many contain sugar. This theme continues in 'The tooth test' where pupils answer questions on the amount of sugary foods they eat and how conscientious they are about their own dental health. The importance of dental hygiene could be emphasised by inviting a dentist or the school nurse to talk to the pupils.

Senses - pages 42-48
The importance of touch is examined. Sound and listening skills are discussed and pupils are encouraged to examine the importance of sound in their daily lives. A tape of ten everyday sounds (e.g. vacuum cleaner, water running down a plughole, a car engine, etc.) will be necessary for 'Using your ears'.

 Children must be warned not to touch each others' eyes.

The way in which the tongue affects speech is demonstrated by some simple exercises, and how the nose and sense of smell affect taste is examined with a taste test.

© 1994 Folens Ltd.

MY BODY

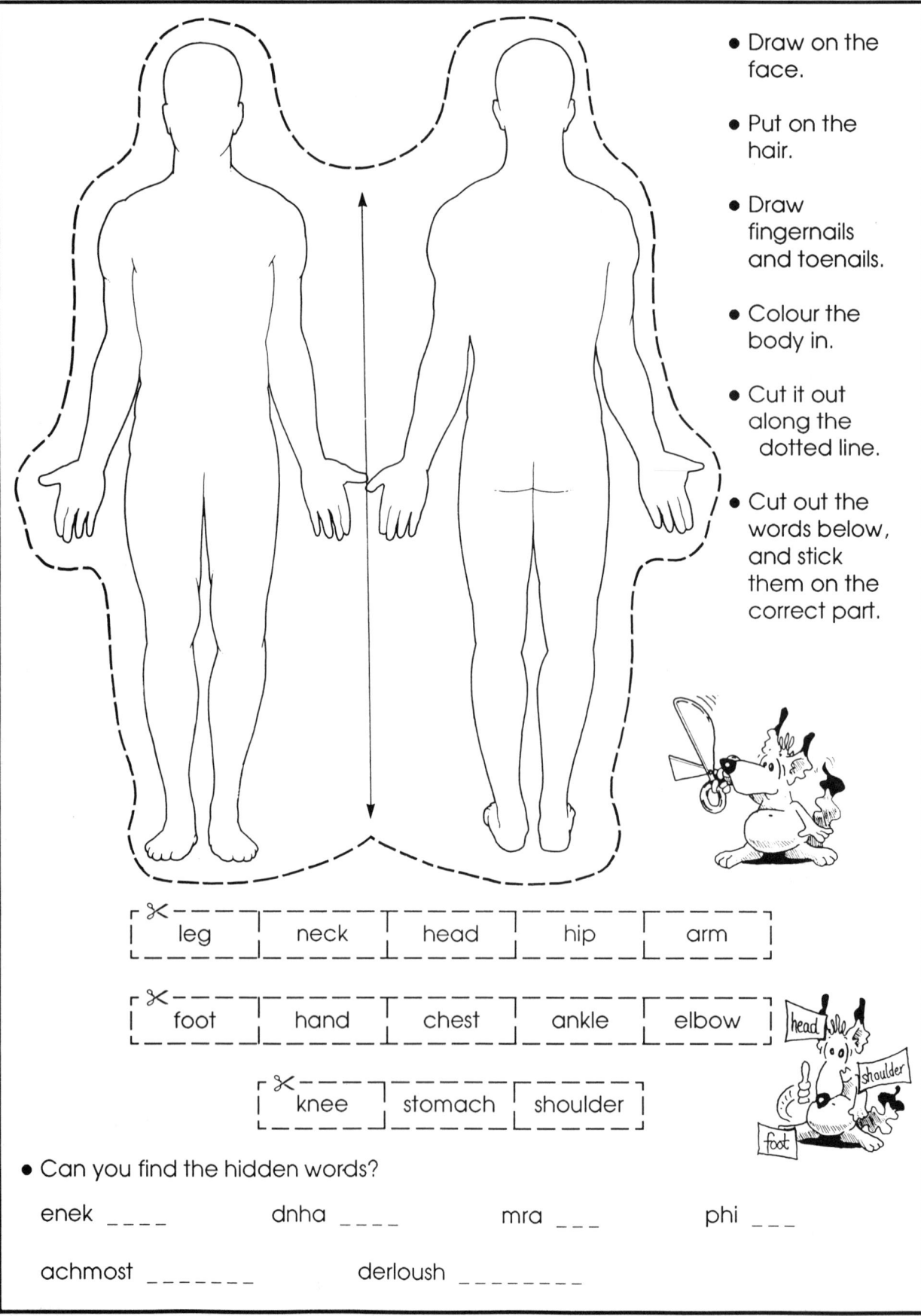

- Draw on the face.
- Put on the hair.
- Draw fingernails and toenails.
- Colour the body in.
- Cut it out along the dotted line.
- Cut out the words below, and stick them on the correct part.

| leg | neck | head | hip | arm |

| foot | hand | chest | ankle | elbow |

| knee | stomach | shoulder |

- Can you find the hidden words?

enek ____   dnha ____   mra ___   phi ___

achmost _____   derloush _____

MY BONES

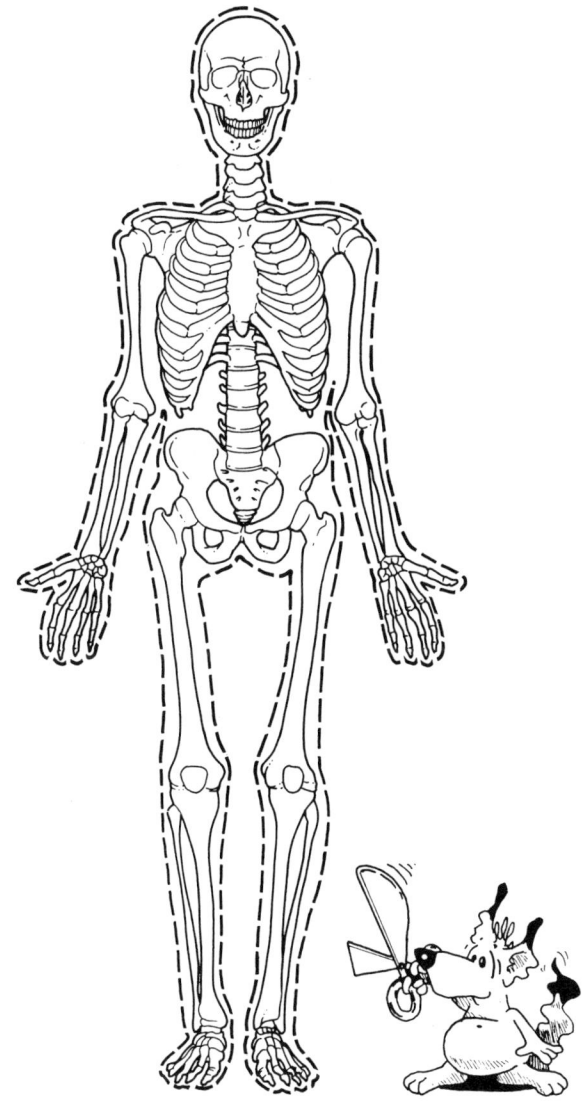

- Cut out the skeleton along the dotted line.
- Stick it inside the body from **My body**.
- Cut out the words below, and stick them on the correct part.

```
hip
elbow
knee
ankle
knuckle
wrist
shoulder
jaw
ribs
skull
spine
pelvis
collar bone
```

- Fill the gaps with the correct words from this list:

  foods; bones; dogs; strong; animals; skeleton.

Lots of animals have _ _ _ _ _.

These bones join together to make a _ _ _ _ _ _ _ _.

Some _ _ _ _ _ _ _ that have a skeleton are _ _ _ _.

- Can you name some more?

You can eat and drink some _ _ _ _ _ that help your bones to grow _ _ _ _ _ _,
e.g. milk, cheese and fish.

MY JOINTS

A joint is a place in the body where bones meet.
There are four different kinds of joint.

1. Ball and socket joint

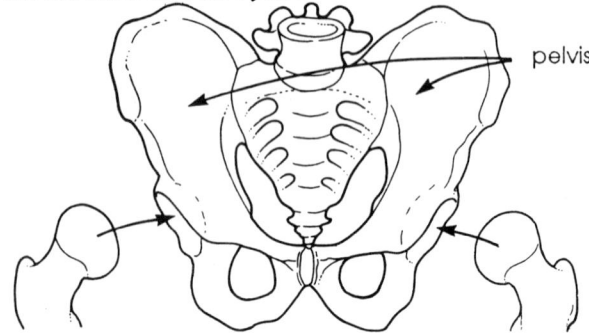

pelvis

A round-ended bone fits into a cup-shaped hole called a socket.

Your hip joint is a ball and socket.

joint
joint
joint

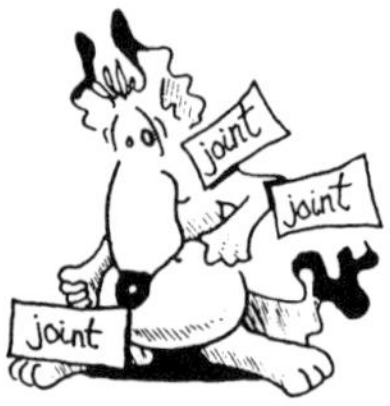

2. Hinge joint

Your elbow is a hinge joint.

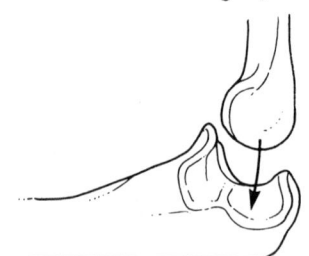

3. Sliding joint

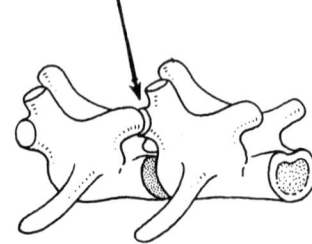

Your backbone is made up of between thirty-two and thirty-four small bones called **vertebrae**. They slide against each other, but only slightly.

4. Pivot joint

Your head turns on a pivot joint.

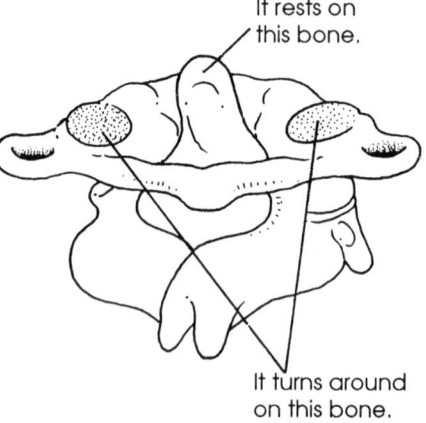

It rests on this bone.
It turns around on this bone.

• Try moving these joints. Fill in the chart.

	sideways	forwards	backwards	round and round
How does your hip joint move?				
How can your elbow bend?				
How do the vertebrae in your back move?				
Which ways can you move your head?				

• Try moving other joints. What kind of joints do you think they are?
• Add them to your list.

WHICH JOINTS ARE WHERE?

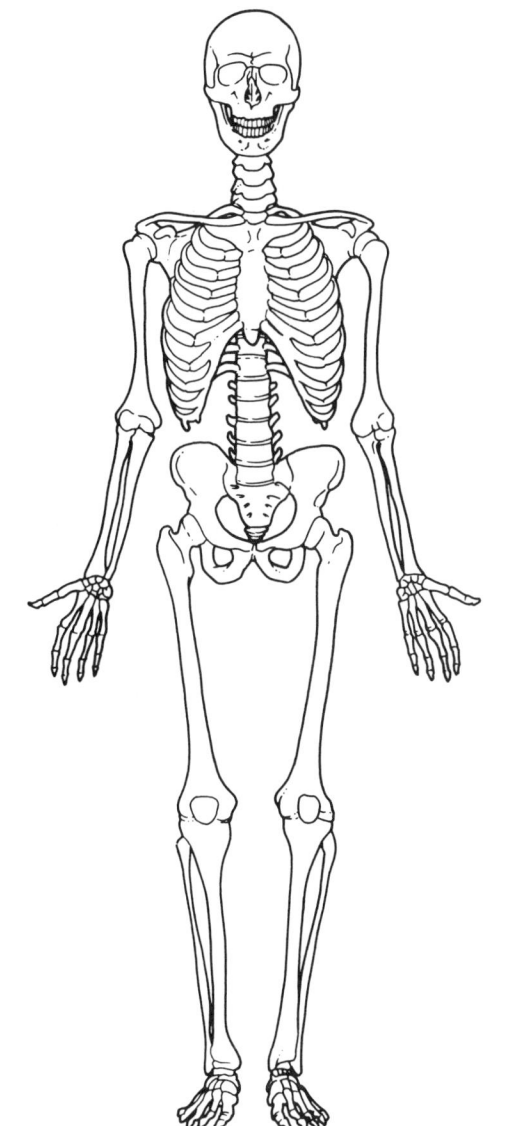

- Can you mark the places on this skeleton where there are joints?
- Put **J** for joint.
- Move the parts of your body listed below.
- What sort of joint have you moved?

	ball and socket	hinge	pivot	sliding
elbow				
ankle				
knee				
finger				
toes				
hip				
vertebrae				
wrist				
head				
jaw				
shoulder				

- Use a washable felt tip pen to mark places on your own body where there are joints.
- How many joints can you find?

- Find some dolls and model figures.
- Make a chart to show which of their joints move like yours.

Which doll	Joints which move like mine		
	elbow	ankle	knee

© 1994 Folens Ltd.   *Getting Personal: My Body* F4171   Page 9

JOINTS I USE WHEN I'M ...

WALKING

- Think about your joints as you walk across the room.
- Use this chart to record which joints you use.

	a lot	some	a little	not at all
ankle				
knee				
hip				
elbow				
wrist				
fingers				
toes				
spine				
neck				
shoulder				

- Check with a friend. Do you agree?

CATCHING

- Pretend you are catching a ball.
- Use this chart to record which joints you use.

	a lot	some	a little	not at all
ankle				
knee				
hip				
elbow				
wrist				
fingers				
toes				
spine				
neck				
shoulder				

- Try other activities, and draw charts to record the joints used.

MAKING A MODEL WITH JOINTS

1. Collect together the things you need: scissors, glue, card, sweet tubes, egg boxes, ping pong balls, wool or string, tape.

2. Draw, then cut out feet, hands, legs and arms.

3. Flatten the sweet tubes at one end. Tape them to the leg and the arm so that they don't bend all the way back. Tape on the hands and feet.

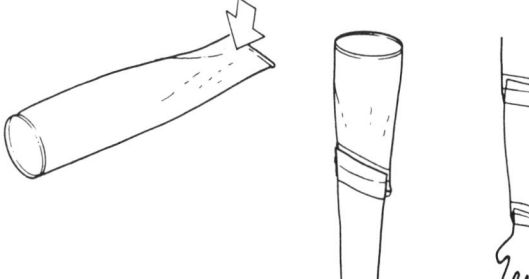

4. Make the hip and shoulder joints (ball and socket) ...

a) Glue the balls to the tubes. Leave them to dry.

b) Cut out 4 egg box cups.

c) Push the balls and tubes into the egg cups and twist together.

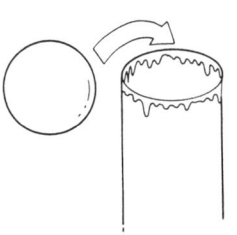

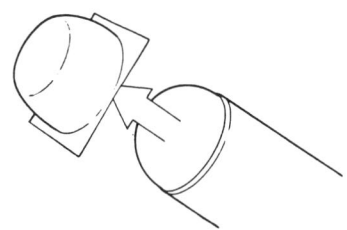

5. Make the head and leave the glue to dry. (You will need to decide on the size of the head.)

6. Make holes in the bottle big enough for the egg box cups. Push in the ball and socket joints and the head.

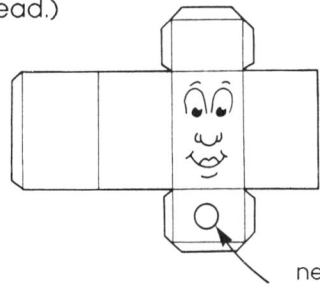

neck

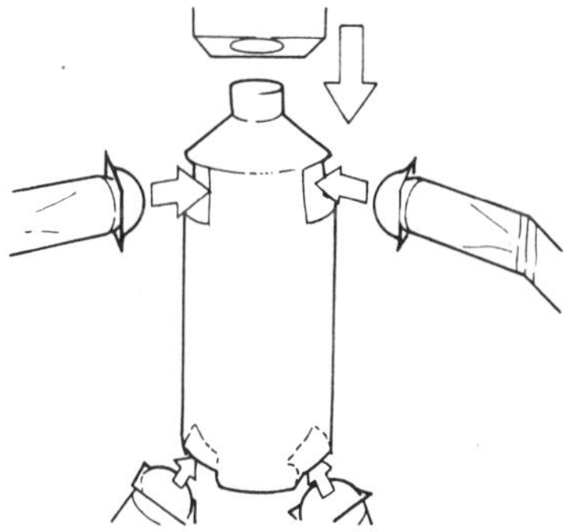

7. Decorate the model and give it some hair.

- Do the joints on your model move like your own joints? How are they different? How are they similar?
- Make a chart to record which joints are similar to yours.

© 1994 Folens Ltd.   *Getting Personal: My Body* F4171   Page 11

HOW YOUR BRAIN GETS INFORMATION

Your brain collects messages from parts of your body and tells your body how to react.

- Connect the labels to the correct part of the diagram.

| SKIN |
| - sensitive to temperature, pain and touch. |

| EARS |
| - sensitive to sound. |

| TONGUE AND NOSE |
| - sensitive to taste and smell. |

| EYES |
| - sensitive to colour, light and movement. |

- Make a chart to show the messages which this girl's skin, ears, tongue, nose and eyes are sending to her brain.

Test your hand and eye co-ordination

1. Hold a piece of paper about half the size of this sheet as high as you can.
2. Let it fall.
3. Try to catch it using one hand only.
4. Do this five times with your left and five times with your right hand.
5. Record your results.

- Is one hand better than the other?
- Did you get better with practice?
- Try to design investigations to test your touch, your smell, your hearing.

YOUR BRAIN

Look after your brain!

Your brain is inside your skull. Your skull is like a bony crash helmet which protects your brain.

Your brain is made up of tiny cells. They can be destroyed by injury, or at birth.

They cannot grow back.

- Why do you think cyclists should wear crash helmets?
- Why do you think you should wear a seat belt in a car?

This picture of a brain shows the parts which look after parts of the body.

- What might happen to someone whose head was knocked in these places?

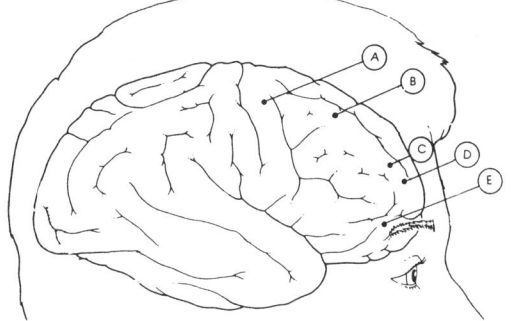

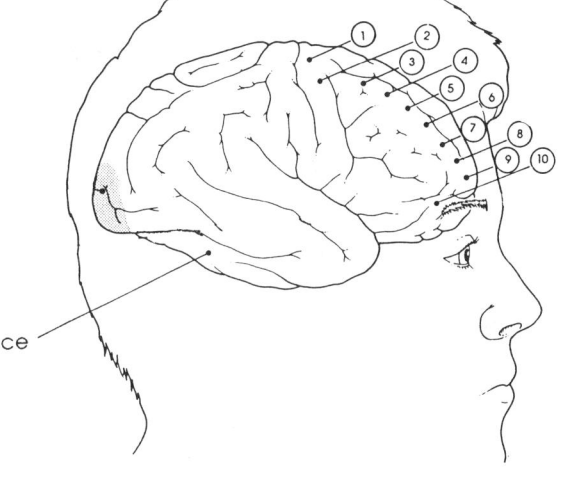

- Copy and complete the chart below.

Injury	Effects
A	
B	
C	
D	
E	

1	legs	6	eyes
2	trunk	7	face
3	arms	8	lips
4	hands	9	tongue
5	fingers	10	speech

In 1982 Bill Beaumont was Captain of the English Rugby team. He was knocked on the head while playing rugby. Afterwards he had trouble seeing properly.

- Explain why this was, using the diagram to help.

HELPING YOUR MEMORY

- Read this list of words for three minutes.

    money   street   snake   pavement   sausages

    shop   lollipop   video game   school   homework

- Cover the words and try to remember them.

- Keep the words covered. List them: _____

_____

- Now try putting the words into a story.
  Picture the story in your mind.

I put some **money** in my pocket and went out into the **street**.	I saw something strange: a **snake** on the **pavement**.
'Snakes don't eat **sausages**,' I thought as I went into the **shop** ...	to buy a **lollipop** and a **video game**, 'nor do they do **school homework**.'

- Cover the page so far and try again to list the words: _____

_____

- How many words did you remember:

    - without the story? ☐

    - with the story? ☐

    Did the story help?

Page 14   *Getting Personal: My Body* F4171   © 1994 Folens Ltd.

MEMORY FUN

- Ask a friend to give you a list of ten words to remember for a test at the end of the day.

- List the words you are given here: _____

- Put the words into a picture story:

At the end of the day, your friend should ask you to remember the ten words.

- Tell your friend the words.

    How many did you remember? ☐

    Do you think word lists are easier to remember if they are linked by a story?

- Explain your answer to a friend.

"A dozen carrots and a box of teabags."

A dozen parrots and a box of teabags.

A dozen parrots and lots of teabags...

A dozey parrot and lots of bean bags?

RESPIRATION

Respiration is when your body gets energy from food.
It happens inside your body.
You need energy to move and even to stay alive.

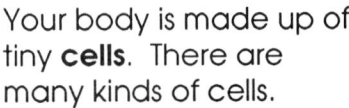
Your body is made up of tiny **cells**. There are many kinds of cells.

1. Each cell in your body needs oxygen to stay alive.

2. The oxygen breaks down the food and releases energy.

3. All cells must be near a blood vessel so that they can get energy from the oxygen.

4. As each cell uses the oxygen to help it get energy, it makes a gas called carbon dioxide (the symbol for this gas is CO_2).

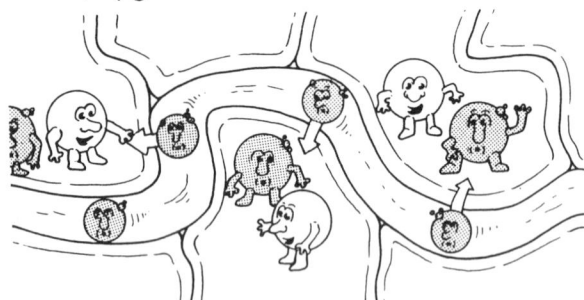

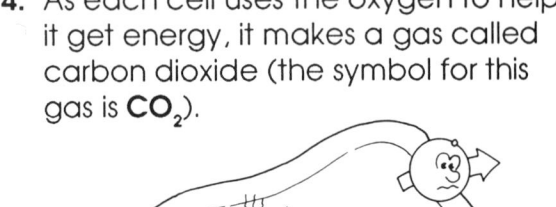

5. Blood vessels carry the carbon dioxide away.

6. Your heart, lungs, arteries, veins and capillaries help this to happen.

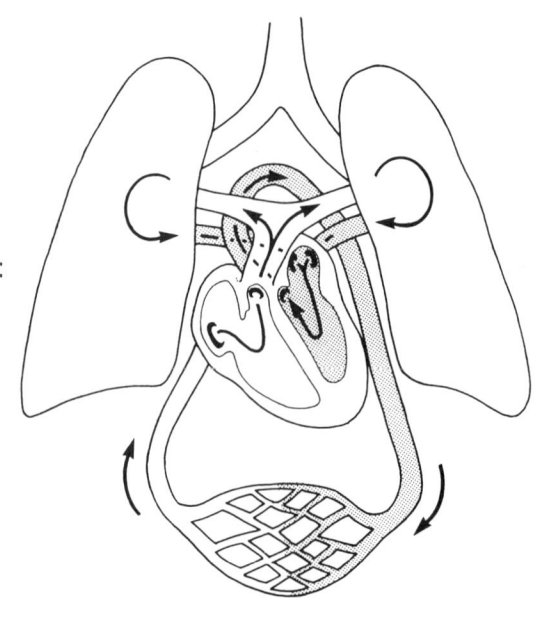

- Try to explain what is happening in picture 6:

   Lungs _____

   Heart _____

   Veins _____

   Arteries _____

   Capillaries _____

MEASURING YOUR LUNG CAPACITY

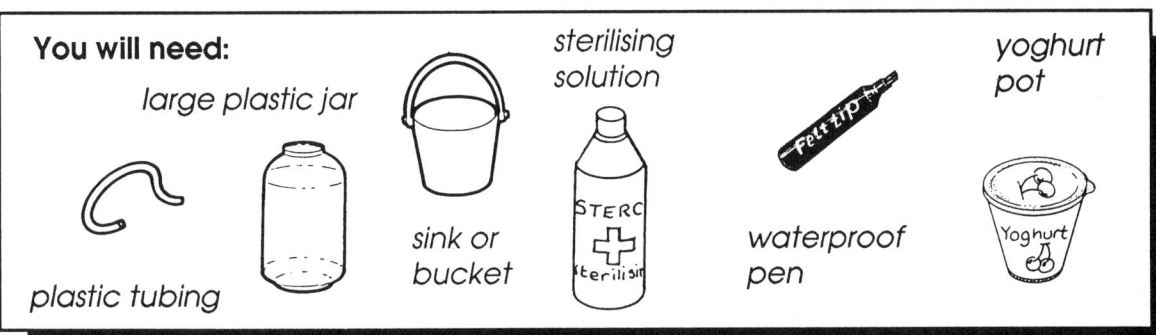

You will need: plastic tubing, large plastic jar, sink or bucket, sterilising solution, waterproof pen, yoghurt pot

How much air do you think you breathe out?
_____ yoghurt pots full.

Find out:

1. Fill a yoghurt pot with water.

2. Pour it into the jar, and using the waterproof pen mark where it comes up to.

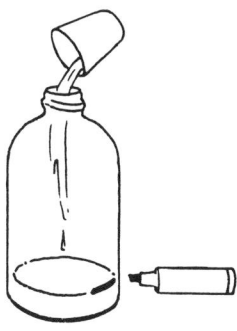

3. Pour in another pot of water.

4. Mark where it comes to using the waterproof pen.

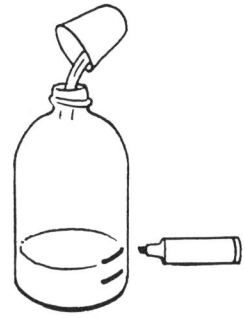

5. Keep doing this until the jar is full.

6. Fill the sink with water.

7. Fill the jar with water and turn it upside down. Make sure there is no air in it.

8. Insert the sterilised tube into the jar.

9. Take a normal breath.

10. Blow out through the tube and notice where the water in the jar goes down to.

11. How much air did you breathe out?

 Sterilise the tube before you use it.

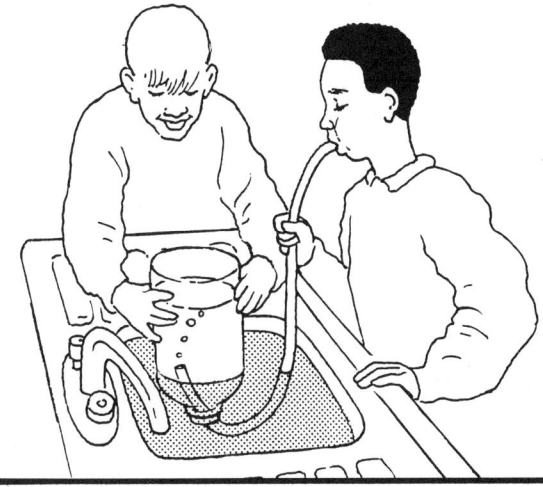

© 1994 Folens Ltd. *Getting Personal: My Body* F4171 Page 17

KEEPING YOUR LUNGS CLEAN

Small bits of dust or pollen can make you ill if they get into your lungs.

Your body has a filter to stop this happening. A sticky liquid called mucus catches bits of dust and pollen. Your nose and other breathing tubes have small hairs. The hairs help to push out the bits caught in the mucus.

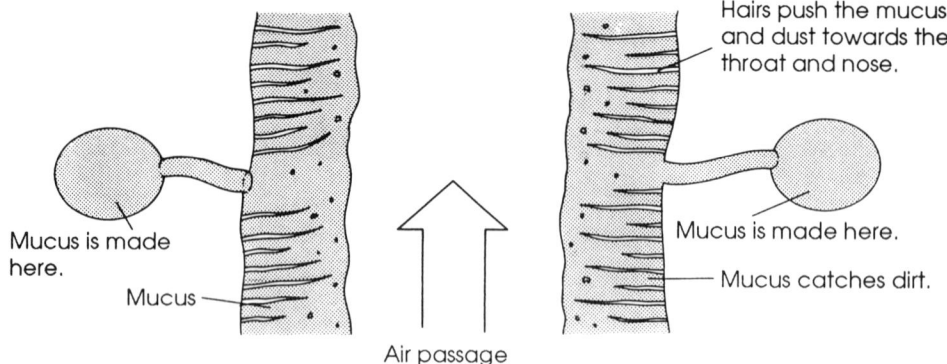

- Find out about filters.
  What do they do?
  What can they be made of?

Investigating filters

- Put the cardboard tube in the tray. Cover the end of the tube with netting.

- Carefully throw a yoghurt potful of dry sand into the tube. (Just the sand, not the pot!)

- How much sand comes through?

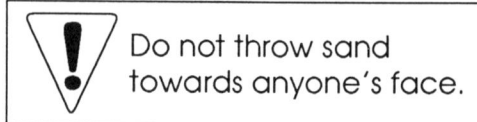
Do not throw sand towards anyone's face.

- Empty the tube of sand.

- Cover the end of the tube with netting which has been smeared with vaseline.

- Throw another yoghurt pot of dry sand into the tube.

- How much sand comes through this time?

- Which was the better filter?

- Which filter is most like your lungs?

You will need:

BREATHING

- Feel your breathing. Put your hands on your ribs and breathe in and out.

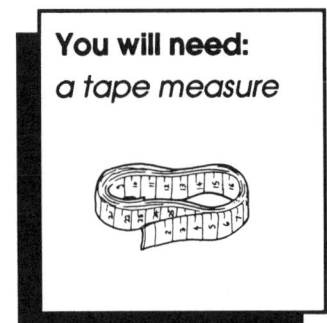

You will need: *a tape measure*

- Which part of your ribcage moves most when you breathe:
  - the top part?
  - the middle part?
  - the lower part?

The diaphragm muscle under the lungs pushes air in and out.

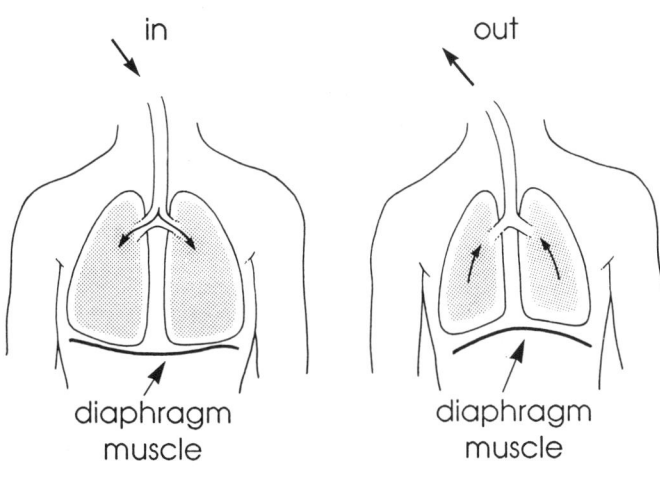

- Ask a friend to measure your chest when you breathe *out* and when you breathe *in*.

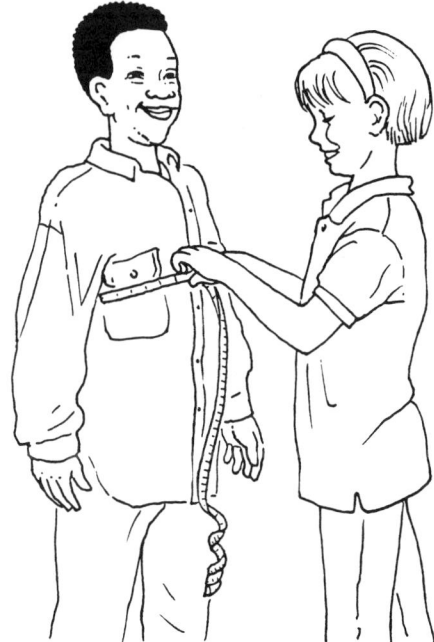

- Record the chest measurements of your group.

Name	Chest measurement		
	Breathing out	Breathing in	Expansion

- Work out the difference in chest measurement. This is the expansion.

- Whose lungs expanded the most?

CHECKING YOUR BREATHING

Sit down and try to breathe normally.

You will need: *a stopwatch*

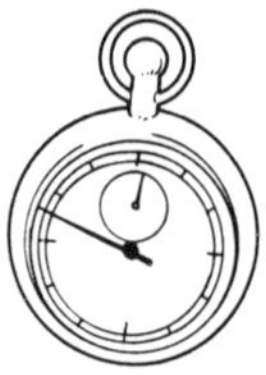

- Ask a friend to time thirty seconds while you count how many times you breathe.
  (Count in and out as one breath.)

- Number of breaths = _____. (This is your resting rate.)

- Find out what happens to your breath after exercise.
- Run on the spot for one minute.

- Ask a friend to time thirty seconds while you count how many times you breathe.
  (Remember to count in and out as one breath.)

- Number of breaths = _____.

- Repeat this after more exercise. (Run on the spot for three, five and ten minutes.)

- Record your results on a bar graph.

Page 20 — Getting Personal: My Body F4171 — © 1994 Folens Ltd.

COUGHS AND COLDS

When you cough you force air out of your lungs and through your windpipe. Coughing helps to blow out anything that should not be there.

- Think of some things which have made you cough:

  _____

  _____

  _____

- What might happen if you did not cough?

- Why should you use a handkerchief?

This diagram shows what happens to the air you breathe.

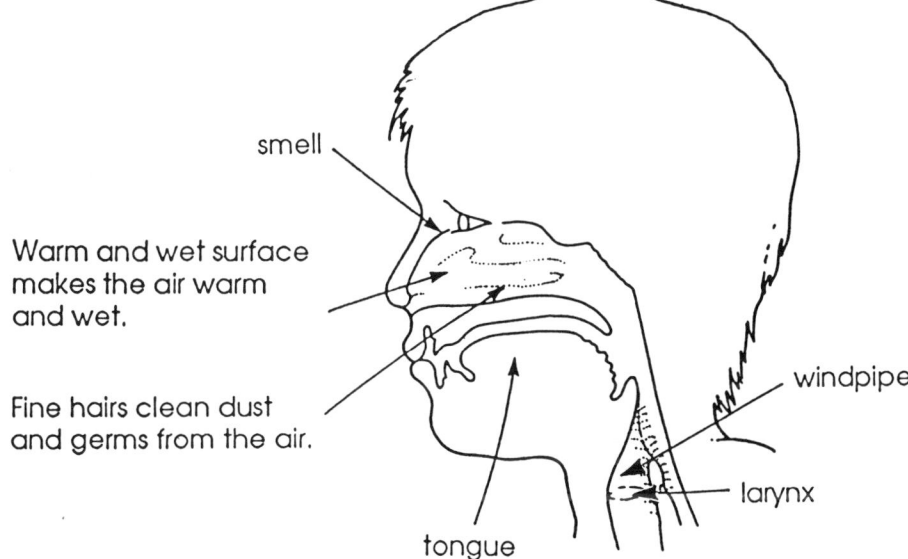

Warm and wet surface makes the air warm and wet.

Fine hairs clean dust and germs from the air.

smell

windpipe

larynx

tongue

- Why do you think it is better to breathe through your nose and not your mouth?

- If you catch a cold, what happens to your breathing?

- If you fall asleep with your mouth open and breathe through your mouth, what could happen?

© 1994 Folens Ltd.   *Getting Personal: My Body* F4171

LUNGS AND SMOKING

You will need: Resource Sheet: Lungs and Smoking

black, brown and green felt tip pens or pencils

glue

scissors

These diagrams show how the air you breathe enters the lining of your lungs.

If the air is clean, your lungs can take in as much oxygen as you need.

- Colour the oxygen supply (the O symbols) green.

If the air is dirty from smoke or fumes it makes breathing difficult.

- Cut out the tar, ash and poison symbols from the resource sheet and stick them on this diagram. Do you have enough room for the oxygen?

- What does this show you?

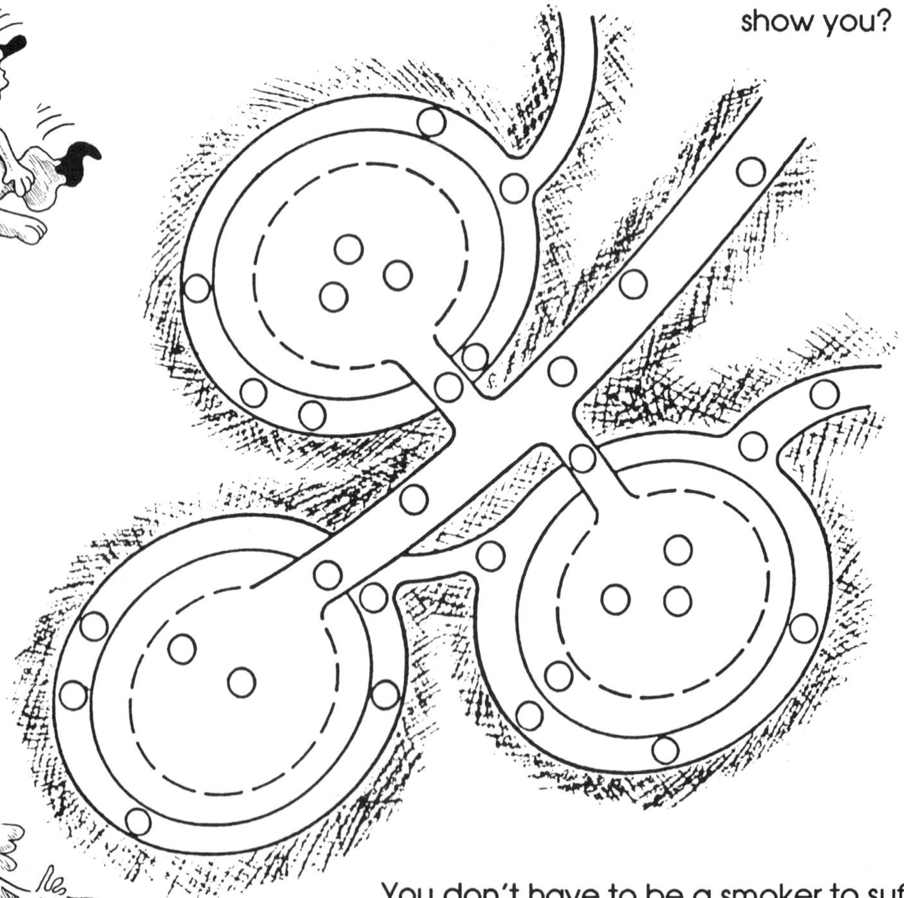

You don't have to be a smoker to suffer from cigarettes.

If you breathe in air that has smoke in it, you can suffer just as badly.

RESOURCE SHEET: LUNGS AND SMOKING

Tar, ash and poison come from cigarettes. Smokers have these substances in their lungs.

Tar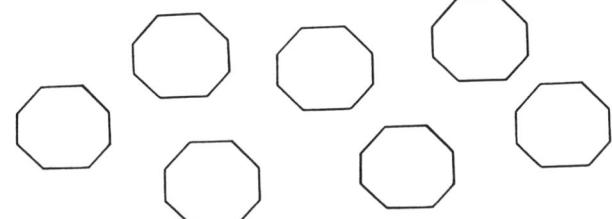

Colour these **brown** and cut them out.

Ash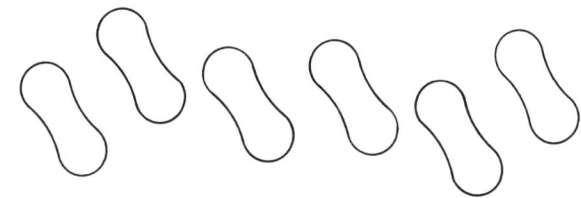

Colour these **black** and cut them out.

Poison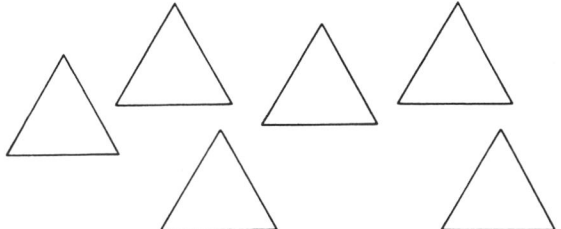

Colour these **red** and cut them out.

- Stick them on to the worksheet **Lungs and smoking**.

- Design a poster to tell others about what you have learnt. Use the message in the box below to help you.

> **Cigarette smoke contains many different substances that can harm your lungs.**

© 1994 Folens Ltd.   Getting Personal: My Body F4171

SMOKING

Some of the words in this story are missing.
What do you think the characters said?

- Fill in the gaps.

- What was Allison thinking in picture 1? Discuss this with a friend.

- How did she feel in pictures 2 and 3? _____
_____

Do you think smoking is harmful?

- Why do people smoke? Write your answer here: _____
_____
_____

- Read the label on a cigarette packet.
  What does it tell you about smoking? _____

_____
_____

WHERE DOES YOUR FOOD GO?

- Use this with the **Resource Sheet: Where does your food go?**

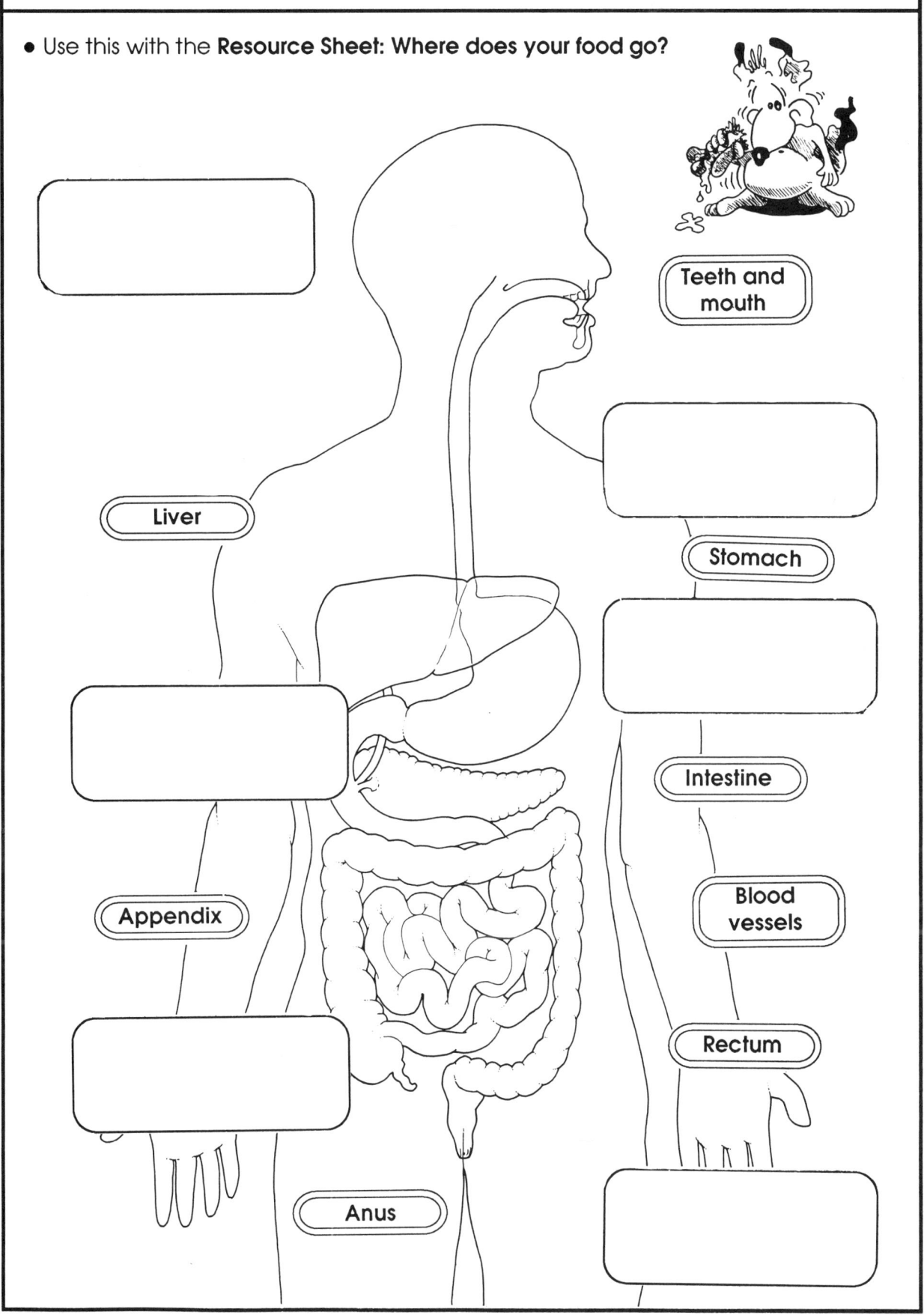

RESOURCE SHEET: WHERE DOES YOUR FOOD GO?

- Copy the sentences in the boxes below into the correct boxes on the worksheet **Where does your food go?**

> The teeth and tongue move food around and pass it down a tube.

> Blood carries food energy to different parts of the body.

> Food is pushed into a long tube. Energy from the food passes into the bloodstream.

> Food arrives and is squeezed and pumped.

> Waste products are passed out at least once a day.

> Food that is not used passes to the rectum.

- Complete this flow chart to show the way food passes through the body:

Teeth and mouth → ☐ → Intestine
↓
Anus ← ☐ ← ☐

- Find out what other animals eat and how they digest their food.

PUTTING YOUR ORGANS IN PLACE

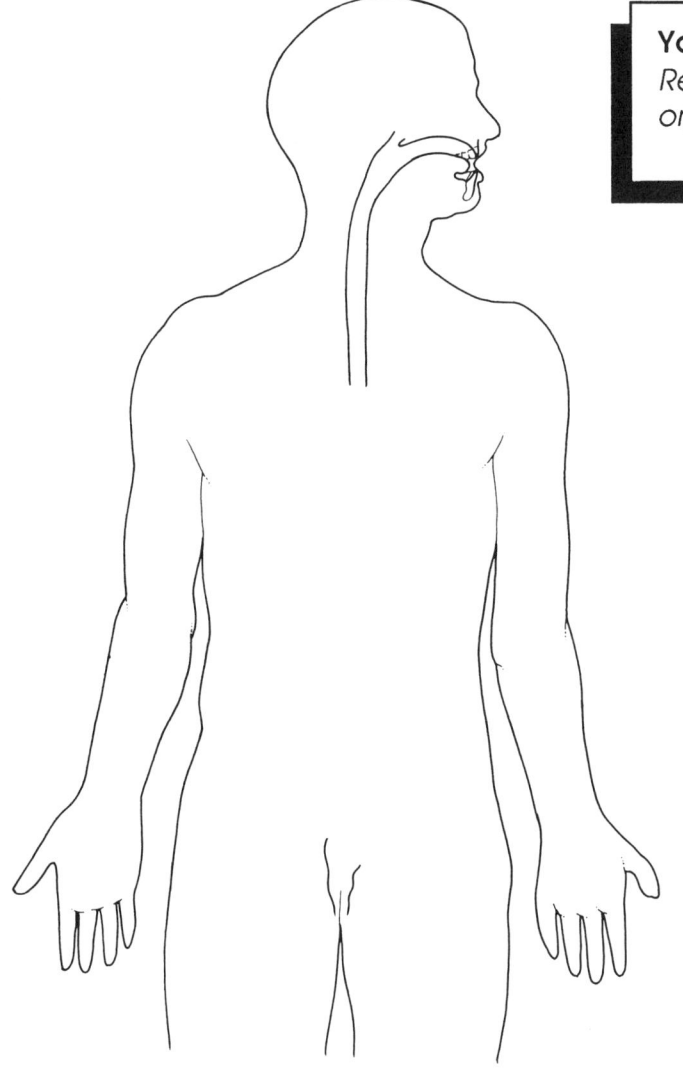

You will need:
Resource Sheet: Putting your organs in place.

- Cut out, then stick the organs in the correct order.

- Cut out the labels and stick them in the correct place.

- Find the missing words.

The st_ _ _ _ _ gets its food from the mouth. In the stomach food is pumped and sq_ _ _ _d. It is then pushed into a long tube called the i_ _ _ _ _ _ _ _. Here the food is passed into the blood where it is carried away to other parts of the b_ _y. The r_ _ _um stores food that is not wanted. Waste products then pass out of the _ _ _ _ at least once a day.

RESOURCE SHEET:
PUTTING YOUR ORGANS IN PLACE

- Cut out these organs and stick them in the correct places on the body diagram on the worksheet **Putting your organs in place**.

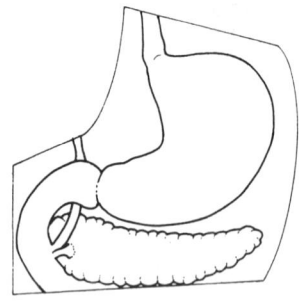 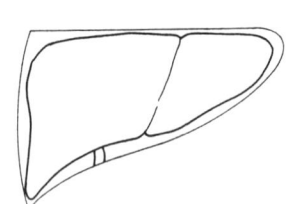

 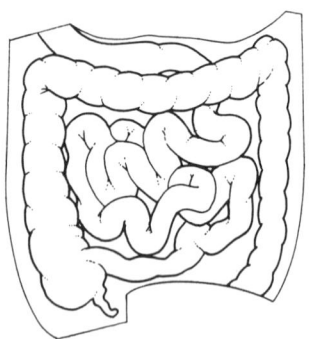

- Cut out these labels and stick them on the body in the correct places:

stomach   anus

liver   rectum

intestine   appendix

CLEANING YOUR BLOOD

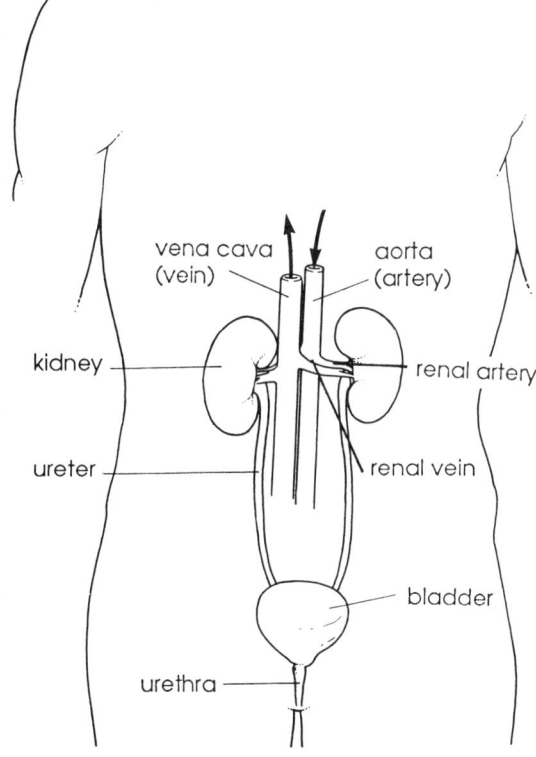

Your **kidneys** *filter* your blood to remove water and other waste materials.

This is happening all the time. The waste (called **urine**) is moved down the **ureters** and slowly fills up the **bladder**. The **urethra** is the tube taking urine to the outside.

Blood is brought to the kidneys through the **renal artery**. The **renal vein** takes the cleaned blood away.

- Complete this crossword:

Across
2) Urine is being produced ___ the time.
3) What the kidneys do to the blood.
5) The tube taking urine to the outside.
7) This takes filtered blood away.

Down
1) The organ which cleans the blood.
2) This brings blood to the kidneys.
4) This stores urine.
5) The tube from the kidneys to the bladder.
6) This pumps the blood to the kidneys.

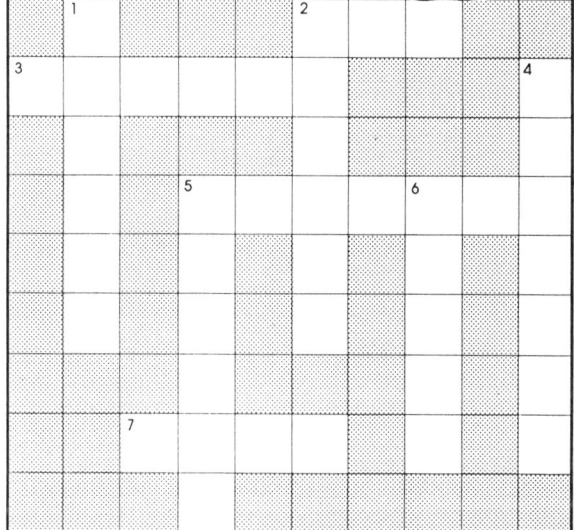

Find out about **filters**.

You will need: *a partner, salt, water and sand mixed together, things to help you separate the sand, water and salt.*

- Think of ways to separate the water, the salt and the sand.

- Plan a fair test to find out which way worked best.

- Record your findings.

YOUR HEART

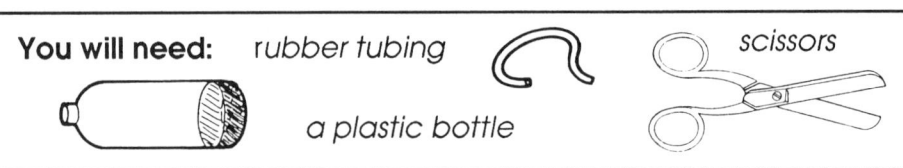

You will need: rubber tubing, a plastic bottle, scissors

Your heart is a muscle. Muscles get stronger the more they are used. Exercise helps to keep your heart strong.
The heart gets energy from food and oxygen in the blood.

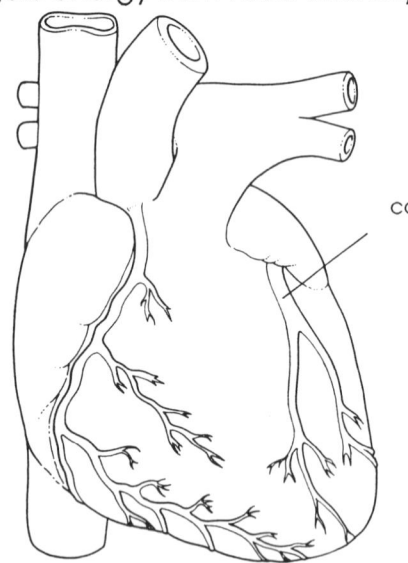

coronary artery

The **coronary arteries** are the main blood vessels to the heart. They supply oxygen and food to the heart muscle.

If the arteries get blocked, the muscle will not get energy. The heart may stop working.

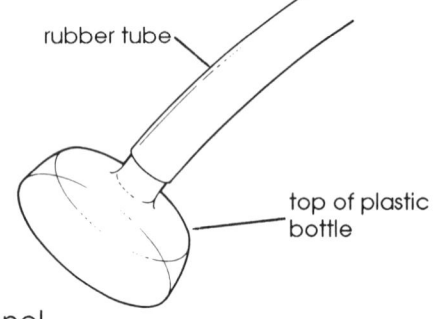

rubber tube

top of plastic bottle

Activity 1
You will need to work with a friend.

- Make a stethoscope.
  1) Find a length of rubber tubing.
  2) Cut off the top of a plastic bottle to make a funnel.
  3) Put the tubing over the end of the funnel.
  4) Listen to each other's heartbeat.
  5) Count the number of heartbeats in thirty seconds.

- You could try just putting your head on your partner's chest and listening:

Activity 2
- Make a chart recording the heartbeats for your group.

Name	Number of heartbeats in half a minute

- What do you notice?

YOUR PULSE

- Find out how exercise affects your pulse rate.

You will need:
a stop clock or stopwatch

- Ask a friend to time one minute while you count your pulse beats.

- How many times did your pulse beat in thirty seconds?
  _____ (This is your resting rate.)

- Run on the spot for one minute.

- Ask a friend to time thirty seconds while you count your pulse beats.

- Number of beats = _____ .

- Repeat this after more exercise. Run on the spot for five and then ten minutes.

- Record your findings on the chart.

Name	Resting rate	Number of pulse beats in 30 seconds		
		After exercise (no. of minutes of exercise)		
		1	5	10

- Test some friends' pulse rates in the same way.

- Record your findings on the chart.

- What do you notice? _____

- How does exercise affect the pulse rate? _____

- Explain this. _____

MUSCLES

Muscles move bones.

When a muscle gets shorter the bone will move.

Your brain sends a message, along the nerves, to the muscle.

The muscle does as it is told! The joints let the bones move.

You do not notice all this happening!

When your arm moves the muscles on top get harder and shorter. The muscles underneath relax.

- Feel the muscles of your arm.

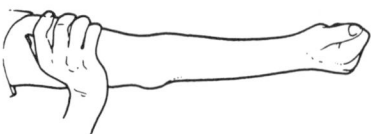

You will need: a tape measure or ruler

- Find out how well your muscles work.

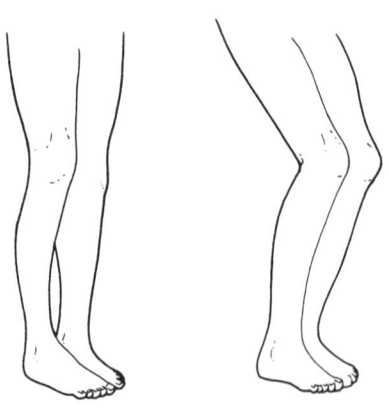

- How far can you bend your knees and still keep your heels on the floor?

Ask your teacher before starting.

- Can you touch or shake your hands behind your back? Try doing it the other way around, with your other arm over your shoulder.

- Ask a friend to measure how far your thumbs overlap.

- Practise these exercises every day. Measure how well you do each week.

	Knee bends measured	Hand shakes Length of overlap (or gap)
Week 1	_____ cm	_____ cm gap/overlap
Week 2	_____ cm	_____ cm gap/overlap

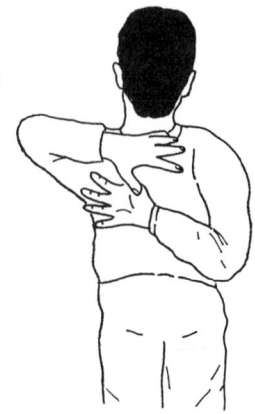

If you cannot reach, measure the gap between your thumbs.

MAKING A MODEL ARM

You will need: *card, scissors, wool, a paper fastener, a hole punch, sticky tape.*

GLUE

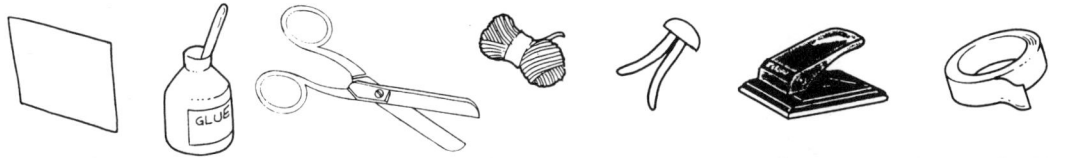

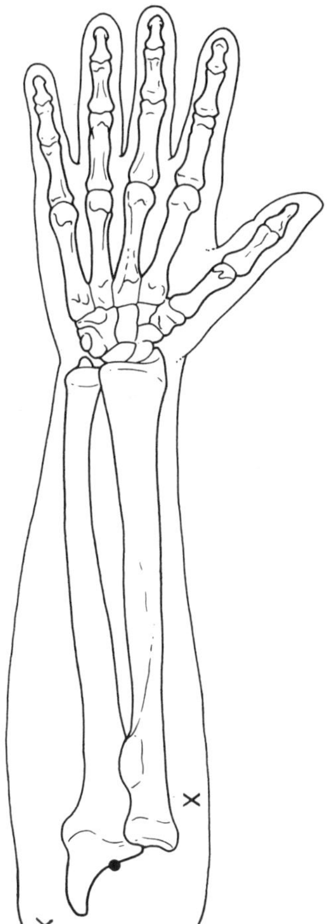

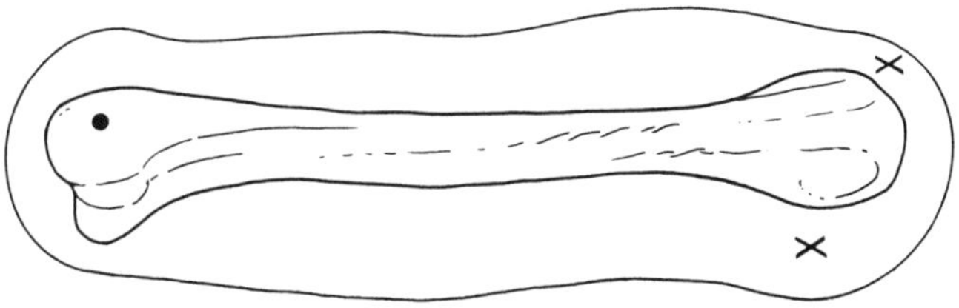

1. Cut out the two shapes and stick them on to card.
2. Put the two black spots together.
   Make a hole through them and fix them together with a small paper fastener.
3. Make four small holes through the **x** marks.
4. Thread the wool through the holes and fix it with sticky tape to the back of the lower arm.

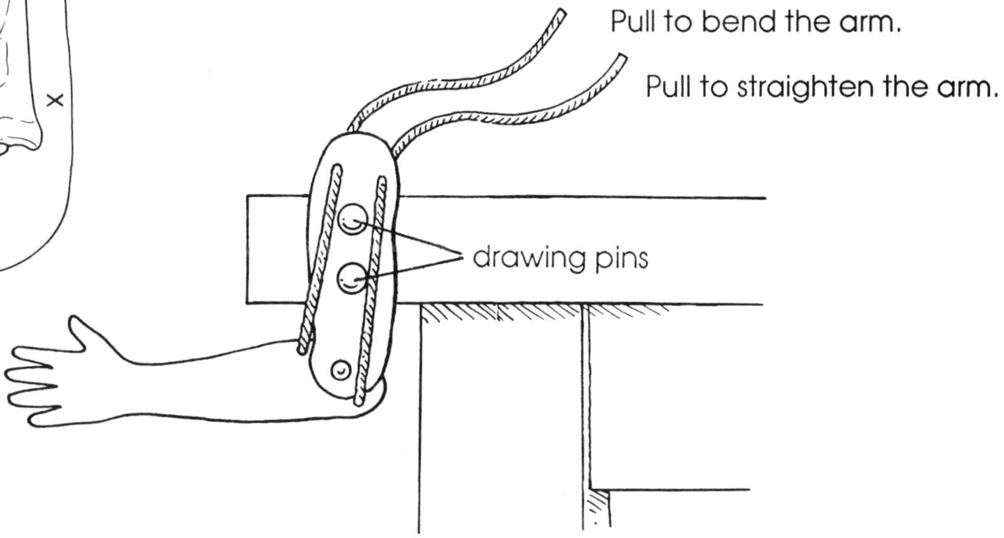
Pull to bend the arm.
Pull to straighten the arm.
drawing pins

Now

- See if you can find out the scientific names for any of your muscles.
- Make a display for your classroom. Draw an outline of your body and label the muscles.

STRENGTH

The more your muscles are used the stronger they become.

 Never try to lift heavy weights. This is dangerous.

Weight lifters train very carefully so that they do not damage their bodies.

- Find out how strong your arms are.

You will need: bathroom scales, two friends to work with

- Push against the scales with one hand.

- Record the reading on the scales.

- Predict the reading for your other hand.

- Test your friends' strength.

- Think about the strongest people you have tested.

- Record your friends' strength.

Name	Scale reading	
	left hand	right hand

How have they become so strong?

FINGERPRINTS

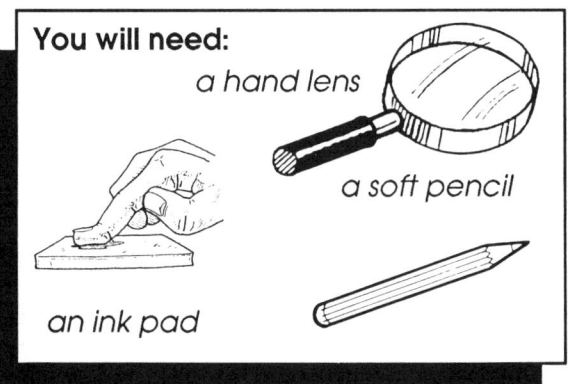

You will need:
- a hand lens
- a soft pencil
- an ink pad

The police know that everybody's fingerprints are different.
They keep a record of every criminal's fingerprints. If they find one of these prints at the scene of a crime, it helps them to find out who has committed the crime.

Look closely at the skin on your fingers, using a hand lens.

Look at your friends' fingers. Can you find any prints that look the same?

Make fingerprints

1. Rub some soft pencil lead on to a piece of paper until you have made a large black area.

2. Rub your finger into the paper until your fingertip becomes black.

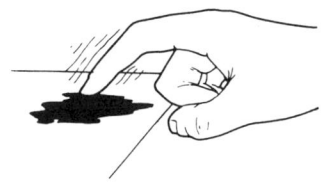

3. Press your finger carefully on to a clean piece of paper.

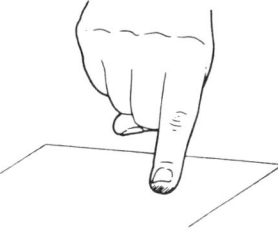

4. You have made a fingerprint.

5. Look at these fingerprint types. Which pattern is most like yours?

loop composite whorl arch

6. Make a graph to show which are the most common in your class.

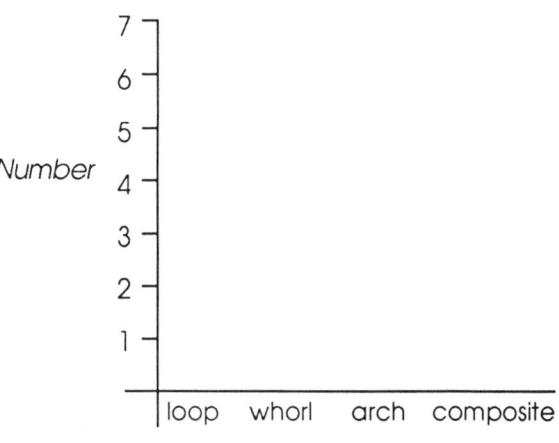

- Try using an ink pad to make fingerprints.

LOOKING AT SKIN

- Make a model of a section of skin.

You will need: *Resource Sheet: Skin*
scissors
coloured crayons
glue

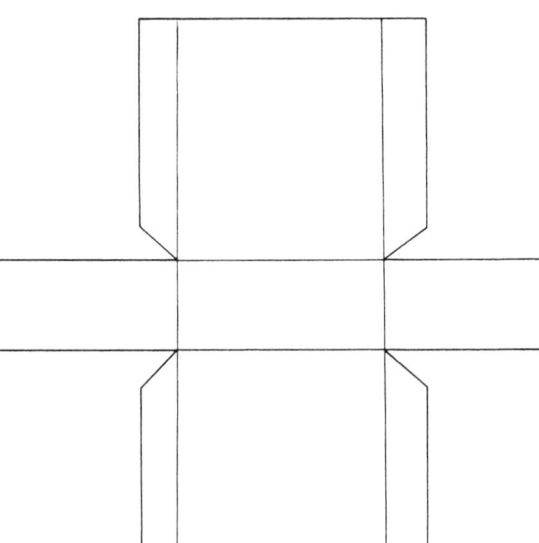

- Colour the blood vessels red.
- Colour the nerves blue.
- Colour the sweat glands yellow.
- Choose your own colour for the surface of the skin.
- Choose a colour for the hair.
- Colour the skin and hair.
- Cut along the heavy lines.
- Score and fold along the broken lines.
- Glue the tabs (to make a cuboid).

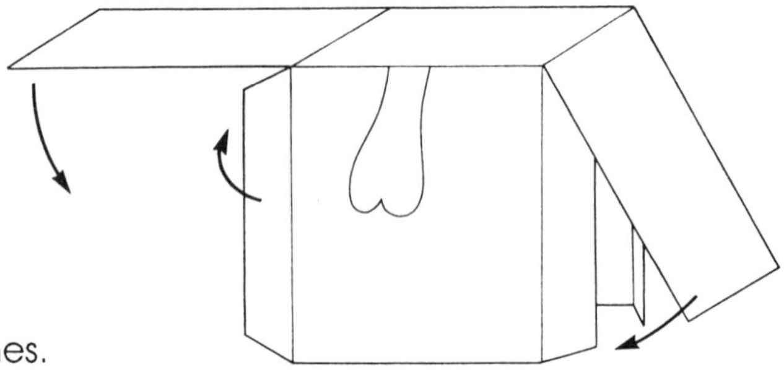

NOW

- Stick the hair on to the hair follicle.
- Cut out these labels and stick them on.

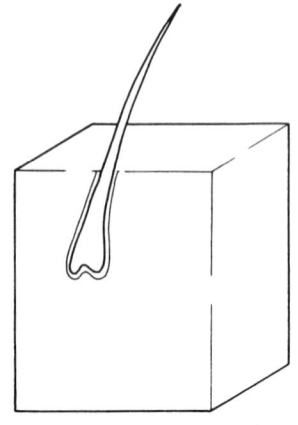

[blood vessels]   [sweat gland]
        [nerves]
        [nerves]   [sweat pore]
        [nerves]

RESOURCE SHEET: LOOKING AT SKIN

- sweat gland
- nerves
- nerves
- nerves
- nerves
- blood vessels
- hair

KEEPING WARM AND KEEPING COOL

You will need:
a hand lens

- Use a hand lens to look carefully at the skin on the back of your hand and arm.

- Draw and describe what you can see.

Find out what happens to your skin when it gets cold.

- Put your hand and arm somewhere cold for about five minutes.

- Look at your skin again, using the hand lens.

⚠ Ask your teacher before you put your hand and arm somewhere warm for five minutes.

- Look at your skin again, using the hand lens.

	cold skin	warm skin
hairs		
colour		
feel		

- Use the chart to record your observations.

- How do you think your skin helps your body to keep warm and to cool down?

Page 38   *Getting Personal: My Body* F4171   © 1994 Folens Ltd.

CUTS AND INFECTIONS

There are germs all around us. Our skin protects us from many germs. They can get into our blood through cuts if we do not keep the cut clean. When this happens, it is called an **infection**. Infections can make us ill.

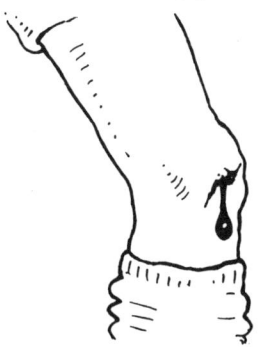

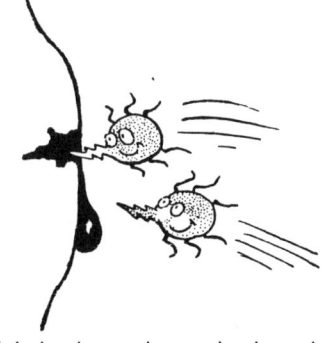

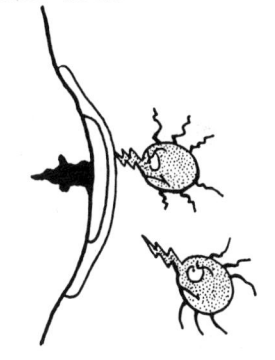

- Look at these picture stories which show how to treat cuts.

A small cut:

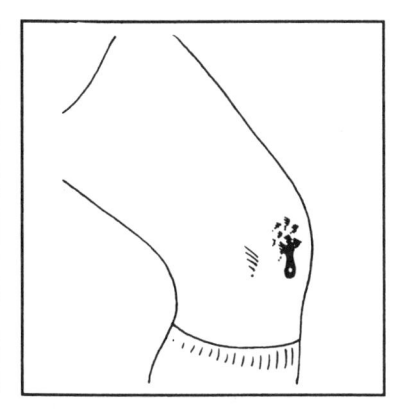

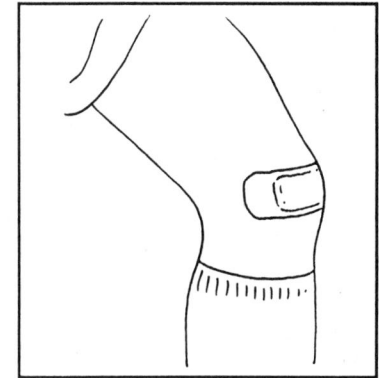

- Describe how the cut was treated.

A large cut:

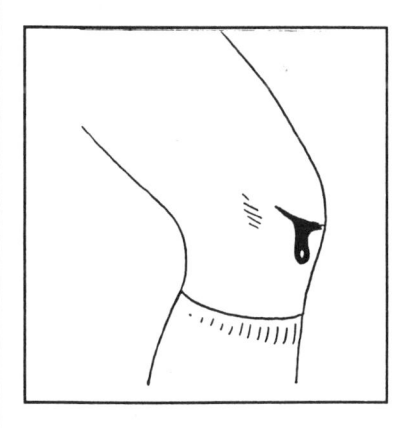

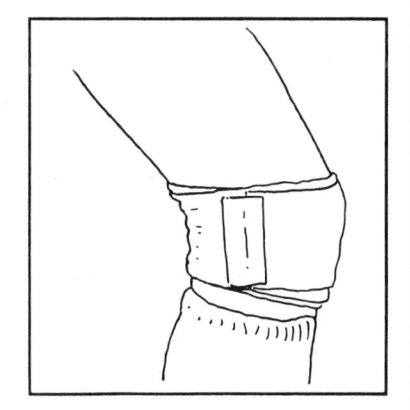

- Describe how the cut was treated.

Keep cuts clean!

TEETH

- Think of some words to describe:

    healthy teeth   **bad teeth**

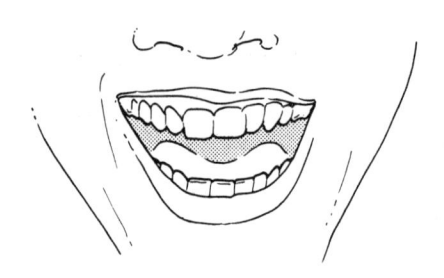

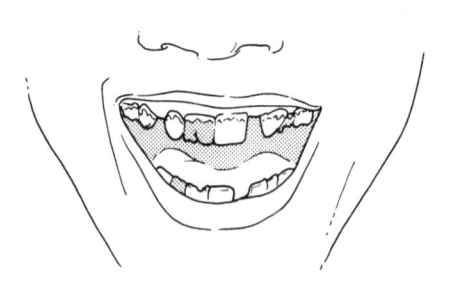

- Now draw and name some foods that are:

    good for your teeth   **bad for your teeth**

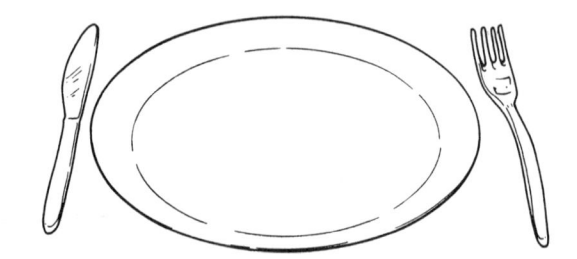

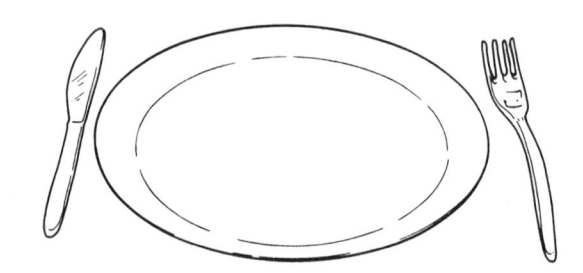

A **carie** is a hole in your tooth. Sugar in your food helps teeth to become unhealthy.
The sugar turns to acid and makes holes in your teeth.
Clean your teeth at least twice a day to get rid of acid and bits of food.

- List five of these foods which you think contain sugar.

- List five which you think do not contain sugar.

- Collect the labels from these foods' packages.

- Read the lists of ingredients on the labels.
  Were you right?

Make a display for your classroom to show which foods contain sugar and which foods do not.

THE TOOTH TEST: WHAT'S YOUR SCORE?

Choose one answer from each set. Record your points.

- I eat sweets or chocolate:

every day	4
less than once a day	3
less than once a week	2
hardly ever	1
never	0
Total	

- I clean my teeth:

once a week	5
once a day	3
three times a day	1
twice a day	2
twice a week	4
Total	

- If I had money to spend on a snack I would buy:

chocolate	4
biscuits	2
orange	1
can of cola	3
Total	

- I visit my dentist:

every six months	1
once a year	2
only when I have toothache	3
Total	

- I get a new toothbrush

every six months	2
every three months	1
every year	3
Total	

- In my mouth I have:

no fillings at all	0
between 1 and 6 fillings	1
more than 6 fillings	2
Total	

- Add up your scores.

- On the drawing (right), colour one tooth black for each point you have scored.

- What does your own mouth look like?

  Are your teeth healthy?

- How can you stop your teeth from going bad?

THE SENSE OF TOUCH

Find out which areas of the skin are the most sensitive.

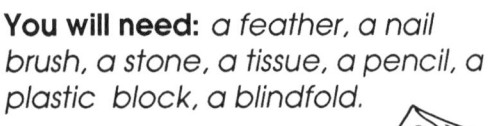

You will need: *a feather, a nail brush, a stone, a tissue, a pencil, a plastic block, a blindfold.*

- Blindfold and test a friend.
- Touch them with each item in the places listed on the chart below.
- Can they tell which item is touching their skin?
- Record whether they are correct.

Part of body	✔ if guessed correctly					
	feather	nail brush	stone	tissue	pencil	plastic block
back of hand						
palm of hand						
back of neck						
knee						
fingertip						
face						
sole of foot						

On which part of their body was your friend able to guess most items correctly?
This is where your friend's skin is most sensitive.

- Test some more children in your class.
- Record your findings on charts.
- Make a graph to show everyone's results.

Where do people seem to have the most sensitive skin?

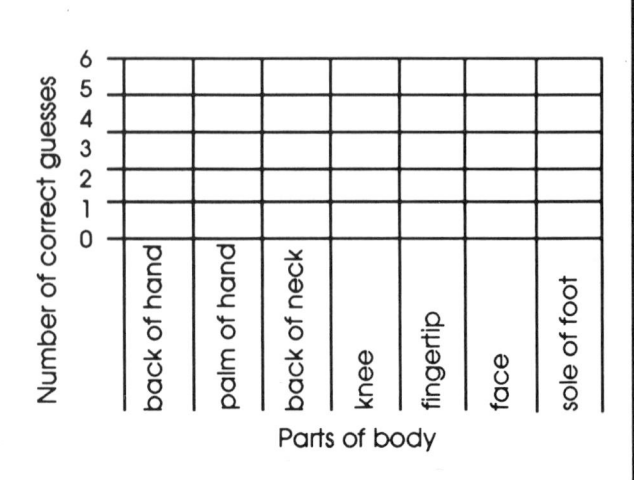

Graph: Number of correct guesses (0–6) vs Parts of body (back of hand, palm of hand, back of neck, knee, fingertip, face, sole of foot)

PROTECT YOUR EARS

Sound is measured in **decibels**. The symbol for decibels is **dB**.
A whisper is 20 decibels (20dB).
Ordinary talking is 60 decibels (60dB).
A jet engine taking off is 140 decibels (140dB).
Noise above 100 decibels can damage your ears.

- Look at the graph. It shows levels of noise pollution.

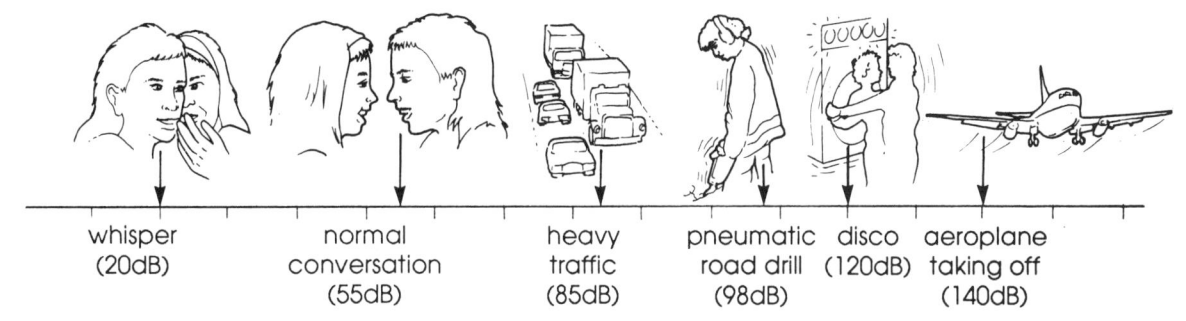

whisper (20dB) normal conversation (55dB) heavy traffic (85dB) pneumatic road drill (98dB) disco (120dB) aeroplane taking off (140dB)

Some children decided to find out who lived in the noisiest place.
They recorded the sounds near their homes.
In school they used the computer to find out how loud they were:

Here are their findings:

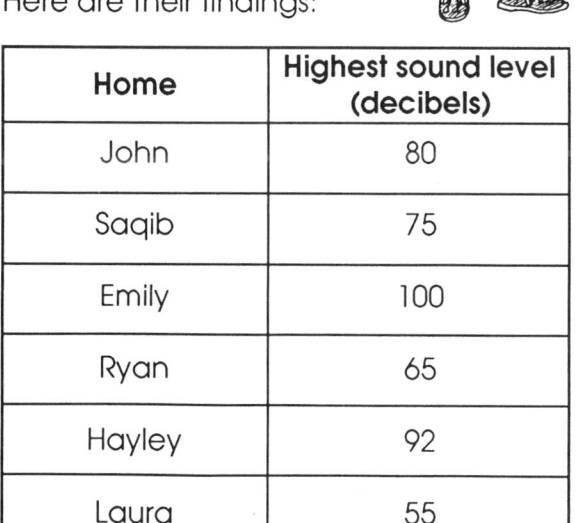

Home	Highest sound level (decibels)
John	80
Saqib	75
Emily	100
Ryan	65
Hayley	92
Laura	55
Guy	60

- Why did they record at the same time of the day?
- Who seems to live in the noisiest place?
- What could stop this test being accurate?
- How could the investigation be improved?
- Discuss your answers in groups.

USING YOUR EARS

Activity 1
You will need a tape recording of ten different sounds. Listen to them.

- Write down on this chart what you think each sound is.

Sound no.	What I think it is	correct ✓ not correct ✗
1		
2		
3		
4		
5		
6		
7		
8		
9		
10		
	Total correct	

Activity 2: Chinese whispers
Work in groups of six to ten people.

The first person writes a message.

The next person reads the message silently.

He or she whispers the message **once** to the next person.

Each person in the circle whispers the message to the next person.

The last person says the message aloud.

Did the last person in the circle say the same message as the one written on the paper?
How many mistakes were there?

- Plan a fair test to find out whether:
  - more mistakes are made if there are more children in the circle.
  - more mistakes are made if the message is longer.

- How could you make sure that no mistakes are made?

LOOKING AT EYES

Do not touch each other's eyes.

Activity 1
- Look closely at a friend's eye. Make a very careful drawing of it.
- See if you can label these: eyebrow, eyelashes, pupil, white, iris.
- How do you think the eyelashes and eyebrows protect the eyes?

Activity 2
- Cut out the pupil size chart below, and hold it just below your partner's eyes.
- Which numbered spot is the same size as the pupil?
  Record this on a chart. The one shown on this page may help.

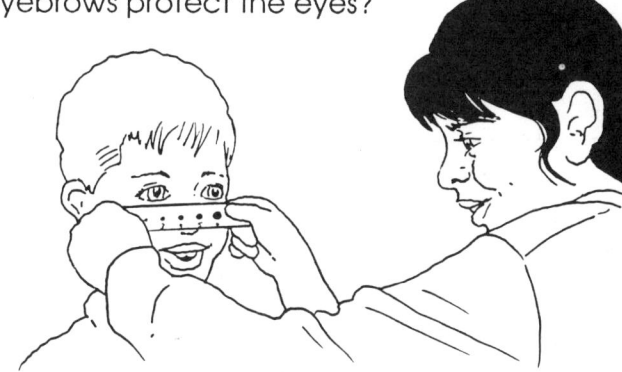

Pupil size chart

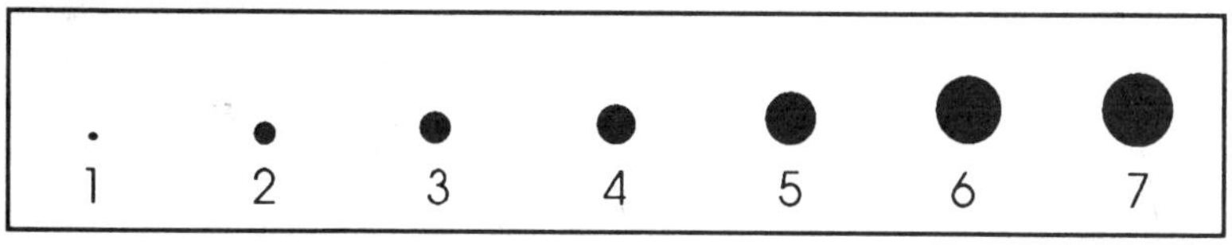

| 1 | 2 | 3 | 4 | 5 | 6 | 7 |

Name	Pupil size		
	Normal	After closing eyes	In bright light

You will need: a torch

- Which numbered spot matches the size of the pupils?
  Record this on your chart.
- Check the size of your partner's pupils after shining a torch (not too bright) into his or her eyes.
- Test some more children in the same way.
- Ask your partner to close his or her eyes, and cover them gently, so that no light can be seen.
- After about two minutes, as soon as your partner opens his or her eyes, put the chart next to the pupils.

How do you think your pupils help you to see, and protect your eyes?

© 1994 Folens Ltd.   *Getting Personal: My Body* F4171

WHY DO WE HAVE TWO EYES?

Try these activities. They may answer the question at the top of this page.

Activity 1
- Close your left eye and quickly try to put a dot in the centre of one of the squares below.

- Now try with your right eye, using another square.

- Using the third square, try with both eyes open.

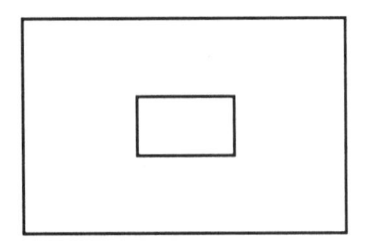

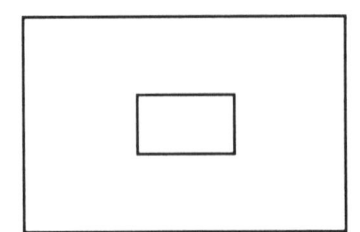

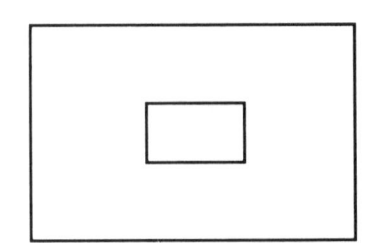

Activity 2
Draw a mark on the classroom floor and stand on it.

1. Look straight ahead.

2. Put your arms out in front of you.

3. Slowly move them sideways until you can only just see them. (Keep looking ahead.)

4. Ask one person to stand on your left, and another to stand on the right.

5. Move your eyes to the left and right without moving your head.

6. Ask both people to move back until you can just see them.

7. Ask them to mark their position on the floor with chalk.

- What do you notice about these positions?

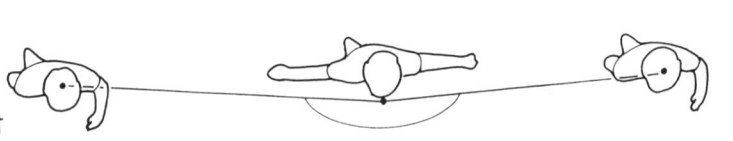

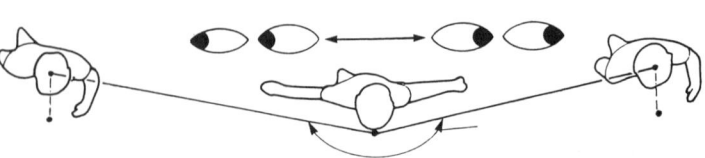

YOUR TONGUE

Your tongue tells your brain what you are eating.

What else do you think your tongue is for?

Find out what it can do!

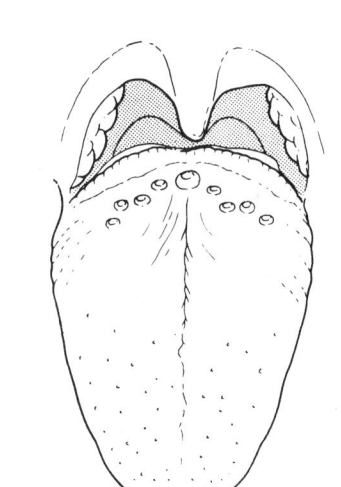

- Open your mouth wide and say "aah" (as you do when the doctor wants to look down your throat).

- Try doing each of these while you say "aah", and notice what happens to the sound you make:

1. Flap your tongue up and down. 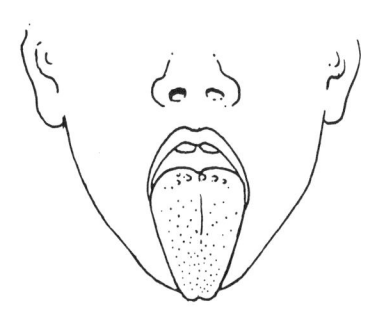
2. Move it from side to side. 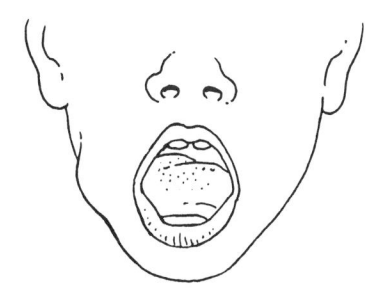
3. Rest it behind your teeth. 
4. Touch the roof of your mouth with it. 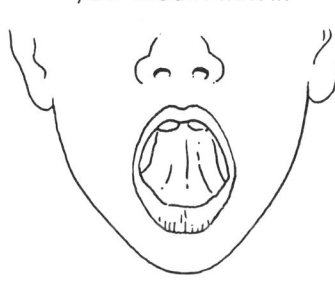
5. Move it in circles.

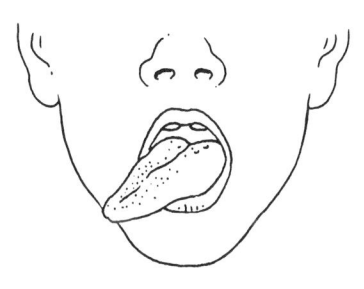

- Say each letter of the alphabet slowly, and notice what you do with your tongue.

- Make drawings and notes to show what you do with your tongue when you say: E, O, R, L, M, S.

- Try saying them without moving your tongue.

Can you roll your tongue?
Do you think all people can do it? Explain your answer.

YOUR NOSE

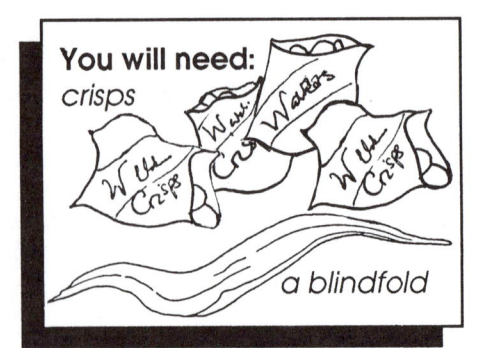

You will need:
crisps
a blindfold

You can usually smell food before you taste it.

- Find out how smell affects taste.

⚠ **Wash your hands before handling food.**

- Blindfold six to eight friends.
- Ask them to hold their noses tightly while you open a packet of crisps.
- Let them take one, taste it, and guess the flavour.
- Keep a tally of the results.
- Next, let them smell the crisps before they taste them.
- Keep a tally of the results.
- Make a bar graph of the results of your investigation.

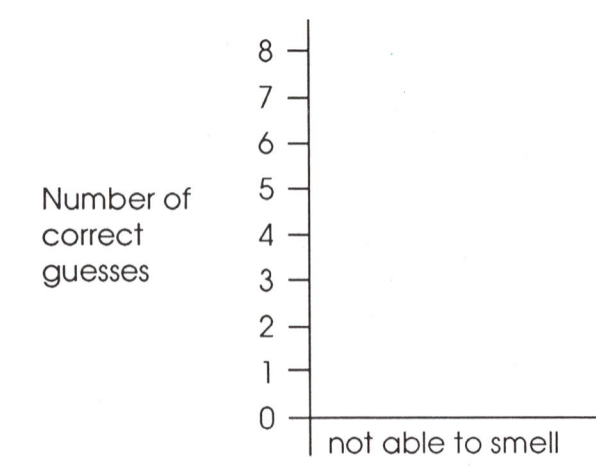

Flavour	Number of children who guessed correctly	
	Tally	Total
cheese & onion		
ready salted		
prawn cocktail		

Number of correct guesses (0–8)

not able to smell   able to smell

- Do you think smell helps you to taste?
- Do another survey like this with children from another class.
- Are the results similar?

Getting Personal: My Body F4171